Social Media Marketing For Beginners

Unleashing the Power of Digital Marketing, Build a Strong Online Presence of Your Business

By: **Blake Preston & Brian Scott Fitzgerald**

Published By: Fitzgerald Publishing Group

How to Make Money Online: THE SERIES

I created a series of 12 (twelve) books on How to Make Money Online.

Feel free to read any of my books in the series, which can be found on my Author page on Amazon at:

You can visit this link or Scan this QR code to get access

https://www.amazon.com/author/brianscottfitzgerald.

Content

Your Free Gift

Thank you for your purchase; I'm offering my readers the FREE PDF…. "The Power of Social Media; Improve Your Knowledge On Social Media."

To get almost instant access, go to this website. https://go.fitzgeraldpublishing.com/opt-in-page-smm-for-beginners

Or use your phone to take a picture of this QR code, and it will take you to the Website for your Gift.

Wait, that's not all; just for buying this book and getting the free PDF above, you can also earn another free Book.

You can use your phone to take a picture of this QR code.

Use the latest AI techniques to uncover online innovation's future. Take advantage! "Beyond ChatGPT and 50 New AI Tools: The Ultimate Guide to Discovering Cutting-Edge AI Tools Beyond ChatGPT" offers endless possibilities. Explore a variety of cutting-edge AI solutions to transform your work. Discover advanced AI tools beyond ChatGPT on this thrilling voyage.

Grab this free book if you want to make even more money online.

Introduction

Hi there, and welcome to endless possibilities with Social Media Marketing. My name is Blake Preston, and with the help of Brian Fitzgerald and Fitzgerald Publishing, I will teach you the reality of social media marketing, which will shift your view of this powerful platform. Discover easy ways to boost website traffic instantly. The idea that all you need is "viral content" is false. Creating content with a focus can increase website traffic.

Instead of waiting for overnight success, use proven strategies to develop your internet profile. Follow our advice to fascinate and move readers. Maximizing your site's potential increases traffic. Suppose a substantial percentage of website visitors buy in the future. People believe this, and I can help you achieve it even if it seems impossible.

Our new ideas might transform your online persona. Imagine using social media viral material to boost website traffic. These clever methods may help find the perfect clientele. Give up paper advertisements and go digital! You should anticipate viral content's consequences on your organization.

Learn how social traffic may quickly deliver successful transactions regardless of platform or credentials. Discover the truth behind these myths. Sad to say, most gurus and experts are wrong.

If you believe any of these views, you should not be surprised if you achieve little despite your best efforts and a substantial commitment of time, energy, and money. The world is new, exciting, and full of possibilities.

A metaphor may help your organization maximize social media. Consider your website traffic a cash flow. You may utilize this metaphor or viral content to explode your social media following. You may lose hope while you seek it.

The suitable mental model unlocks social media marketing's full potential. You can enjoy maximum convenience with our cutting-edge autopilot methods.

New "set it and forget it" methods are sweeping the world. These needs likely interest you. They picked the correct brand name. Discover the unique potential of social media marketing automation! Automation technologies make internet presence optimization easy. One-click can reach more individuals, stimulate their curiosity, and boost your chances of success. Switching from email alone simplifies ads. The secret to limitless riches is passive income. Planning may help you achieve your financial objectives.

Enjoy efficiency without sacrificing passion. Our tips and techniques might help you overcome any challenge. Stop striving for more and appreciate your achievements. We guarantee success with our unique processes. Refrain from settling for mediocrity when you can shine bright.

Each new concept and powerful brushstroke might make you look accomplished. I hope you are receptive to change as we happily and carefully assist you in developing and polishing your thinking.

Consider the significance of your message—set goals. Believe in your freedom of expression. An inverted pyramid will demonstrate social media marketing's attraction. Excellent funnel form. Use a metaphor to increase your social media following.

Turn social networking into cash. Consider the appeal of an inverted pyramid. Let this fantastic idea enter your mind; the world is your oyster. The new design centered on a large foundation. Only the pyramid's peak offers these tremendous views. Spread compelling information on the top four social networks to get fans. Use cutting-edge digital choices wherever feasible.

It would be nice to understand and notice your target audience. We will assist you in incorporating social media into your business. Famous social media networks Facebook, Twitter, YouTube, and Pinterest are fantastic. Millions of people worldwide are drawn to these digital titans' unmatched powers. You may meet new people, debate intriguing issues, and obtain endless creative ideas.

The astonishing figures on these four social media sites will wow you. Learn how these sites and others can draw massive crowds.

Your success will increase after employing our unique tactics. The road to greatness and fame begins here. Your site will attract visitors and possibly sell if you succeed.

Since our concepts are ageless, they may be applied to different mediums. Asset enhancement allows subtle enhancements. With our help, you may customize them to your liking. Let your creativity and abilities shine. Make use of Instagram's versatility and marketing possibilities. Share our professional advice on social media to understand how these basic concepts may increase your Instagram presence.

Social media has a considerable reach. People may not click on internet content. Discover the legend's truth. Major networks offer unmatched coverage.

Sharing across platforms boosts content visibility. Discover the wonderful Facebook sharing secret. Some people who see your link in your friends' posts will click it.

Discover why increased Facebook "reach," or exposure, doesn't automatically mean more clicks. Fresh thinking that challenges traditional wisdom. Use a unique strategy to win. Change your mindset and recognize the future's potential. The first step in a new effective process is to enhance content exposure across all platforms. Flaunt your individualism; you must. Showcase your efforts. International expansion may boost your reputation.

Visitors to your site will be more engaged. Even if it's not the focus, a click-through is unmatched. You can profit from our skills and doors. Discover how our unique techniques may enhance your company and personal life. Come on for this fantastic experience with us as your dependable travel companion.

Discover internet visibility secrets. Knowing this is vital. Want to maximize it? Want more and better exposure? It may get fewer visitors. You read this book because you recognize it's more than it seems.

Consider getting intrigued by an advertisement. How recently did you click an ad without thinking? The ad may take many viewings to "get it," as many do. Take the marvelous throne. An intriguing commercial or ad may grab attention.

Social media success depends on memorable content. Increase your internet presence to attract people. Use social media to communicate and interact. Tell captivating stories to differentiate your business. Discover how to use social media to get thousands of visitors.

Popular headlines and photographs are essential, but they cannot guarantee success. It doesn't work that way, which is surprising. I've never felt uncomfortable writing and distributing great work that inspires action.

Maximize Your Internet Presence.

One-click may transfer your viewers to a thrilling new realm. Help others show their gratitude by visiting your YouTube channel, clicking "like" on Facebook, "following" you on Twitter, or "pinning" a post. Use this opportunity to rivet listeners! Enjoy the dialogue when site visitors subscribe or follow you.

The second level of current social media marketing funnels is an inverted pyramid. Building platform trust is crucial to success. Expertise is advised.

Our help can speed up your expert status. You may grow your consumer base and wow your target audience. It's too intriguing and well-meaning to write randomly. It's a masterpiece made to attract your audience. This particular material preserves your talent and individuality.

Use captivating images and content to market your business and stand out. Because of its uniqueness, consumers will remember your brand even if they don't click on your ad. Discover repetition's advantages. Your firm will gain visibility even if a tiny portion of your audience interacts with your social media postings.

You need to provide engaging material to maximize social media accounts. After grabbing their attention, use the "call to action" info. Use your email list to test it. Be memorable to your specialty. Email marketing firms should be joined. Take advantage of this unique chance to gain new consumers and fans. Sign up today to gain subscribers. Find fascinating social content with attractive prizes.

Learn what makes your product or service unique. Amazing freebies like booklets or software are always accepted. Freebies, webinars, and fun online presentations are available. Always prioritize recruiting exclusive group members. The epic "The

Endgame" emphasizes forethought, competence, and tenacity. Your goal may be to attract people to click and buy your adverts. Give it your all.

Utilize this social media opportunity. Imagine being invited to an exclusive club. Imagine your previously dispersed online audience becoming loyal and enthusiastic—list membership peaks when the pyramid is turned upside down. Enjoy converting social media admirers into moneymakers.

In this surreal world, the impossible is common. The unlikely and strange are common in modern culture. In-person, the dazzling performance will be unforgettable. Amazing things await you beyond this door. Squeeze pages that promote mailing list signups can boost revenue. People offer you their email addresses because they trust and want to work with you. How to protect and strengthen love. Send them your best content, and stay in touch.

A new view on relationships that values transparency, thoughtfulness, and commitment. The spam-free era of direct touch has begun. Watch out for the guest who messes up your list as we bond.

Consider how your tone and words affect your audience. Words and actions can stir up trouble. Keeping your comments updated helps them understand. Imagine completely controlling your list's sales, engagements, and conversions.

Discover how seven-figure list marketers make money only from mailing lists. Using lists effectively is essential to success. Discover why selecting repeat customers carefully pays dividends. See your carefully chosen list of smash sales records. How well you utilize your list depends on its quality and attractiveness.

There are several ways to turn a large social media following into loyal clients. This meaningful unlocks social media marketing's full potential. Other social media marketing books provide several strategies. These books wrongly claim that a substantial social media following is enough by equating web ad clicks to monkeys' random actions—a safer way to cross this challenging region.

Find something that can boost your progress daily. Our advanced techniques can help you work faster. Why settle for mediocrity when you can excel? Make a complete 180 today for a brighter future. Many marketers might use some advice. Create something unique. Our method will amaze and change your viewpoint; you'll never make mistakes again.

The less-than-ideal truth must be learned. At this stage, many business owners quit. They send social media followers to a sleek landing page to promote their content. Unique material and rewards on squeeze pages keep people coming. Too much good may require addressing.

Unfortunately, marketing wastes many prospective subscribers. New email users must know the terrible truth: be prepared for anything. Want a unique vacation? Surviving the unexpected requires preparation. These people have boundless learning and advancement potential. It may take some employees time to acclimatize to our strict criteria. See these people grow in ways you wouldn't expect.

Look into their experiences—you may be shocked. See how their talent improves the item. Let me present the worst individuals who will astound you with their capacity to push limits and relax.

Learn the importance of a brief list. Why waste time with a vast roster when a lean, efficient team would do? Thin, profit-generating networks replace resource-hogging list squatters. If you choose quality above quantity, you can make more monthly.

Preventing list bouncers and improving service are smart. Welcome a population that registers for your email list for your tempting premium offer, downloads it, and leaves without opening it. You eliminated them well.

Effective Social Media Marketing

Advertising via social media might help you stand out more. Promoting your company with engaging content that strengthens connections with your audience is efficient. Social networking sites might completely revolutionize your company and bring you unimaginable prosperity. The speed with which beneficial relationships may be converted into outcomes is greatly enhanced by social networking. Spread the word using your email list.

Our state-of-the-art method of email list creation lets you lose on precision. I use selected social media content to craft artwork based on your promotion efforts. If you target the right people with your ads, you'll see a considerable increase in responses. Get the best social media marketing outcomes available.

Social Media Marketing: a Revolution

Step into a world where every piece of information, story, and photo that is proudly published online becomes a beacon, drawing in customers quickly. Discover the truth about digital and social media advertising. Which is more exciting? Unleash your tremendous might!

See how quickly things change in the digital realm. Join the hundreds of thousands of new social media users every day. Get to know individuals who share your passions and expand your knowledge. Use the many willing people who have tried your products to your advantage. The right strategies can help you capitalize on this invaluable resource and expand your business.

Learn how to make meaningful connections with others. Learn the transformative potential of one-on-one contact. Learn the potential benefits of close relationships. Learn the magic of connecting with others.

Learn more about the human connection captured by social media. Find out how to raise your online profile's visibility. It would be best if you rethought the way you approach content. Have faith in your methodical technique and give up on luck. Real connections with the audience are successful. Tell brand and personal tales to pique their interest. There is such a thing as resonance magic. Social media's influence is unprecedented. Get your message out there and create an encounter that will make people care about what you're doing and want to spread the word about it.

Take advantage of the Domino Effect!

Picture a fascinating pebble in your writing. Your material's power will slowly permeate social media, sparking a massive uptick in attention and discussion. As the flood of likes, comments, and shares sweeps over the web, it sounds like a symphony. Don't be surprised if your sway eventually extends beyond your devoted fan base to the general public. This excellent book contains game-changing strategies. Be astounded when your brand's message spreads from a trickle to a flood. Get ready for massive growth and remarkable achievement.

Unleash Creativity

Has the constant change in social media algorithms worn you down? Don't let defeat get you down. As a savvy marketer, you have earned the right to keep and expand your online presence. Please assist us in deciphering and utilizing the algorithms of social media. I help you overcome obstacles and succeed in the digital world by providing the necessary resources.

Make use of numbers and figures in your marketing strategy. Real relationships, genuine content, and open participation are the three pillars of effective digital engagement. Including these foundational elements will increase the likelihood of your message being heard and remembered. Capture attention and spark interest in your product. Step into the spotlight in a world ruled by algorithms. If your readers enjoy and trust your posts, no algorithm will be able to outrank you. Engage with customers and other business owners to expand your company.

A wonderful self-discovery experience.

This is a captivating tale unlike any other. A journey of profound self-discovery and exploration awaits you on every page. If you can crack its code, you'll get access to a wealth of information that will alter your life irrevocably.

Act authoritatively and clear the way. Marketing in the social media era is a must. Feel the revitalization of your brand like never before. Our fresh perspective will excite listeners and stimulate growth in the economy.

Think Creatively

Every product line has a unique history that contributes to its uniqueness. Make use of marketing on social media. Keeping an audience interested is essential while narrating a narrative. Benefit from the revitalization of your brand thanks to the vital connections made possible by social media.

The revolutionary changes in marketing will soon astound you. Help me usher in a new era of advertising by coming along on this incredible journey. Expect ground-breaking concepts, mind-blowing originality, and brilliant advertising. Things in marketing are going to heat up. This book unlocks the secrets of social media advertising's enormous potential.

Do you have the innovative resources, astute methods, and expert understanding to rule social media marketing? Get ready for an adventure that will alter how you approach marketing, making connections, and growing professionally. Buckle up because you're in for a ride of a lifetime. Be led by a revolutionary revolution.

Chapter 1

Social Media Marketing – An Overview

The Digital Revolution Awaits

Prepare for an exciting adventure into the Digital Revolution. Prepare for limitless possibilities and groundbreaking advances. Take advantage of the future. Embrace

Enter a domain where your tweets, posts, and stunning images transcend the fleeting digital universe. Each sentence becomes a masterpiece that captivates the public by turning ordinary words into exceptional expressions. It seamlessly guides thousands of eyes to your brand, messaging, and visionary goals. Enter social media marketing and be amazed by its revolutionary potential!

In the digital age, social media is powerful. Unleash the power of billions of users on Facebook, Twitter, Instagram, and Pinterest. You'll be amazed by the reach. The ultimate secret to unlocking social media's full power: a skill few have but holds the key to extraordinary success. While most people use social media, only a few know how to maximize its potential. Start a remarkable journey here.

Discover Social Media's Untapped Potential

Be fascinated by the stories of brands going viral overnight. Prepare to be amazed by postings with millions of shares. And prepare to be amazed when ordinary people become internet stars. This collection of stories will surprise you. Despite being genuine, these tales only touch the surface. Explore the immense ocean of potential beneath the surface. Prepare to dive into unlimited possibilities.

But let me explain. This is not about viral trends or short-term stardom. Discover how to build lasting relationships, create a captivating brand presence, and use social media to interact with your audience.

Launch Your Brand's Potential in a Revolutionary Marketing Era!

Enter the future of marketing, where billboards and TV ads are obsolete. Your target audience is captivated by internet platforms in today's fast-paced digital world. They effortlessly scroll through their feeds, avidly devouring content that matches their interests and passions. They engage with digital content that speaks to their hearts and minds, from fascinating films to thought-provoking posts. And what makes it great? Direct communication, meaningful dialogues, and a vibrant community around your great brand are possible.

Unleash your exceptional potential. Accept your immense power because it comes with a great responsibility. This incredible power comes a world of unlimited possibilities and a huge responsibility. In today's noisy digital environment, noise is everywhere. The internet is packed with posts, tweets, and videos in a 24/7 digital environment. Are you ready for the final test? Raising your voice in the noise ensures your message reaches and resonates with your audience.

"Social Media Marketing for Beginners" Will it help if you are fed up with being stuck and unclear about how to succeed? Look no further! "Social Media Marketing" is here to help.

This chapter will take you on a beautiful journey to understand social media marketing and provide an overview. Learn how to write articles people want to read again. You should deliberately choose material that will engage your followers like never before, not merely publish on your page. It's about more than contacting everyone. Learn that social media is about connecting with others, not simply following.

To succeed online, you must overcome your limiting beliefs and adopt the strategies that have made the most successful companies. Discover the intricate science and art of creating appealing content. Release your vital techniques to increase your voice and influence. Discover hidden gems that turn readers into brand evangelists. Expect an interactive, persuasive learning experience.

Discover life-changing journeys' endless possibilities. Your amazing adventures will enchant you. Once you make that daring move, you'll discover who you are and grow. Consider all the fascinating travel prospects. Imagine your brand having a more profound influence on your audience than visibility. Imagine a large, rapt audience listening to your every word. Imagine a company-changing marketing approach.

Prepare for a fascinating trip via deep comprehension, powerful strategies, and extensive information. This primer covers everything you need to master social media marketing. A fantastic voyage into social media advertising awaits! I feel like a revolution is happening!

Clear up social media advertising confusion. Explore the intriguing world of social media marketers, where every perspective and interpretation matters. The reading options will amaze you. Learn about social media marketing, where several disciplines form a unique online environment.

Content, navigation, or social media expert? Everyone has an online strategy. Some focus on the network, others on exciting content. Then, there are some with meaningful relationships. Your distinctive opinion, regardless of your side, will stand out online.

Use social media marketing's untapped potential to engage your target audience. Discover how I can explain this complicated environment to help you achieve. Use the changing digital world to grow your network, influence, and wealth. Join this exciting adventure to discover social media's advertising power.

Do you require additional explanation? Fully comprehended. Don't worry—it's typical. When I'm confused, I try to explain. By accident, I'm focusing on tiny aspects to boost traffic.

Discover why many internet marketers and company owners fail at social media advertising. Discover the incredible potential ahead. When something happens, it works. A good definition is essential to project success. Without it, obstacles may arise.

Limiting expectations opens many doors. If you fail, try again—victory against obstacles. Realizing your potential requires accuracy. The correct definition may alter your life. Align yourself precisely and clearly to succeed. Always choose the best while preparing for the future—experience how a detailed explanation may lead to success.

Victory Secrets in a Winning Definition!

Discover the amazing world of social media advertising and how it may benefit us. This revolutionary list marketing course will teach you how to monetize your social media following! Prepare for a trip where social media marketing revolves around fascinating content that builds lasting relationships. Prepare to see how content can build long-term audience relationships. Social media marketing is a versatile tool that personalizes interactions with your target audience through engaging content.

Make use of Strategic Advantages.

Can you fascinate certain groups and make genuine connections? Master communicating with your target audience and keeping those critical connections. Find a relationship that transcends words and alters you forever. Change your definition of love and commit forever. Make a relationship real. Only your mailing list needs your attention now. Discover the thrilling challenge of email list growth.

Be ready for the grand finish—everything has been built to it. Expand your network to maximize its possibilities. Create an engaged, contributing group. Social media marketing may generate new subscribers without any effort. Having a list changes everything. Prepare to be revolutionized by this remarkable gizmo. One item that will shape your social media activities.

Management of Expectations

Are you sick of life's disappointments? Now stop! The best answer is my words. A unique social media marketing strategy that will change how you communicate with your target audience through content and interaction. Give up paper advertisements and embrace digital marketing. Social media advertising is best learned from classic books like "How to Dominate Twitter." Learn how to keep visitors coming to your website.

Discover the terrible truth: counting makes you think more is better. While reasonable, this thinking may leave you feeling despondent as the day ends, significantly if traffic doesn't grow. Despite the success, more is needed. The breakthrough social media marketing method of using content to engage audiences.

You want to win over your target audience with relevant, helpful, and exciting content.

This game will transform your life. Marathon running is a testament to tenacity. The sprint tests willpower and commitment to the limit. Drive yourself to new boundaries with each mile and enjoy the race. Not racing, but the tremendous experience every stride brings. Set ambitious goals immediately to succeed. Avoid being the following social media marketer who goes in unprepared and gets no visits. Explore their knowledge to discover extraordinary possibilities. Master their craft and see their revolutionary results. Their incredible talents will amaze you when they cast their spell.

Focusing on definition unlocks the capacity to control expectations. Surprises and thrills await you on the path to calm and fulfillment. Rather than typical, you'll stand out. Change your mindset and anticipate with joy to open many doors. Remember to underestimate the difficulty; be positive.

Since you understand social media marketing, I can focus on content-based relationship-building. Discover how to differentiate your brand. The thing that changes everything for you.

Relive real-world driving excitement. Moderate visitors get plenty of light from my modern infrastructure. Prepare for fantastic city culture and nightlife. Try real-world traffic! A distinctive, engaging, and convincing brand may boost your bottom line. Use a solid brand to attract and keep customers easily. Build a legacy. Active learning, not passive browsing.

Find varied folks who love your product. Discover their insatiable curiosity. They want to know the planet's secrets. They're information junkies.

They want to know you and your character out of curiosity. They want to see your affluence and try your products. They want you to believe your cause is unstoppable. This collection of people is excellent. Develop a powerful brand to grow your business. With a big name, possibilities are endless, and I will help you gain an incomparable advantage.

Imagine achieving your goals with content marketing alone. Learn that such statements, although sincere, are false. Discover the exciting reality under the surface. The resolution illuminates inevitable consequences, but much remains unknown. Expect insight as we explore the character. Absolutely! You need engaging material to keep your audience. After joining your elite club, people anticipate and deserve outstanding value.

Learn branding best practices. See the significant shift when people subscribe to your list. Expect to enjoy their time with you. Expect regular, high-quality upgrades that enhance their lives without effort. Social media marketing may boost brand exposure at unprecedented speeds. Discover cutting-edge social media advertising! However, the excitement shows that many need help building credibility. Most of their findings could have been more accidental.

Our most significant hidden discovery will wow you. Discover how content-driven campaigns may improve audience engagement. The upcoming chapters will explain this equation's complex sections so you may understand it. Prepare for an intriguing trip through word meanings and shocking reality. Let this passage's beauty overwhelm you. Follow our detailed project definition.

Setting realistic objectives may help you avoid self-criticism. Never accept less than your due. Develop an attitude that lets you accomplish without self-criticism.

CHAPTER 2

Reasons Why Social Media Marketing is Essential

If you still need to figure out social media marketing's importance, let me give you eight persuasive reasons why it's essential to your online marketing plan. Discover the power of a balanced marketing plan. I understand the importance of both search engine marketing and outreach.

Add social media marketing to your online marketing plan to boost it. It's the missing component that completes your approach and increases brand value. It must be seamlessly interwoven into the composition, not just an afterthought or overshadowed by other considerations. Discover the power of social media marketing with these eight convincing reasons, just a taste of the many benefits your company, regardless of size, will get.

Learn about social media's unmatched power. Social media may boost your message directly and through virality by connecting people globally.

Create a captivating Facebook page to maximize its influence. Directly connecting with your target market has unmatched benefits. Make your page powerful! Discover your extraordinary potential as a select fraction of your loyal followers see your intriguing updates. Discover the truth: Facebook is actively reducing page organic reach.

The latest breakthrough: a fantastic method that effortlessly overcomes all difficulties. You may steer visitors to a more engaging experience on your page. Encourage them to like your page and discover the hidden gem in your page's settings—the ability to prioritize updates. By doing so, they'll never miss a beat and keep current on your engaging material.

A fascinating video lesson that seamlessly walks viewers through the process is the perfect way to engage and educate your audience. Release your imagination and enchant your audience with an animated gif. Discover the key to keeping ahead! Discover how to prioritize updates and always catch every beat. Unlock your settings' hidden potential and take control of social media.

Tell your friends and followers they may join the privileged group that gets your updates first. Remove the darkness and illuminate the way to perfect visibility! Discover how to grab attention and spark curiosity. Your material must be enticing to engage. Be confident and in charge. Discover the appeal of actual value that will attract your readers and get them to act on your website. Instructing others might boost your direct reach.

A revolutionary feature elevates your material! Imagine that people may easily share your content with their whole network if they love it. This could affect your reach and influence. Prepare to see your content fly, spreading like wildfire over many walls. Unleash organic sharing and watch your content go viral! Facebook's social ties are robust. The possibilities are unlimited with friends who have friends.

Expect an astounding exponential impact. Discover the incredible power of genuine connections! Imagine having a few hundred likes on your page, but they're not ordinary likes. There are actual people with natural social groups. Prepare for the day when one of your postings goes viral, engulfing the internet. Prepare to be amazed!

Discover how social media combines habit and fascination in a compelling dance. Expect to be captivated by this digital world where scrolling, liking, and sharing are second nature. Join the seductive social media rhythm, where every click and swipe.

Discover the exciting world of social networking, where various demographics exhibit unique usage habits. Some may say that daily, weekly, or monthly participation has weakened, but the truth is that many people still use social media regularly. Discover the extraordinary morning practice that many follow.

Start your day with modern convenience. They grab their sleek phone or tablet before sunrise, eager to explore unlimited possibilities. They stay in touch with the newest news and updates with a swipe. Start the day with technology and stay informed. Discover how easily it becomes a daily practice.

Unleash the power of engaging content to put your brand in front of millions of hungry eyes.

Captivating Target Audiences

Those elusive individuals crave content in many intriguing ways. Yes, my reader, these people have a particular taste for diverse information consumption. They desire content that speaks to their souls unimaginably, from exquisite writing to compelling graphics that paint a thousand stories.

Break free from a single content type and unleash social media marketing's power. Celebrate infinite creativity and captivate your audience with a variety of intriguing content. Social media marketing holds as many possibilities as the digital horizon. Be creative without limits! The possibilities are unlimited for intriguing films, breathtaking photographs, engaging links, thought-provoking blog articles, appealing text, and captivating audio recordings. Let your imagination soar and create memorable content! Explore a universe where platforms flourish in their formats.

Create appealing content on one platform and quickly translate it into captivating versions across numerous formats to increase your reach across multiple platforms.

Imagine carefully weaving words into an engaging blog post that resonates with your readers. Imagine sharing this literary gem on Facebook, where your words can fascinate and inspire a large audience. With innovation and social media, the possibilities are unlimited. So, release your inner wordsmith and watch your blog post fly on Facebook's limitless potential. Introduce a captivating image to make your blog content stand out.

Enhance your Facebook page with attractive photos! Watch an image teaser draw your viewers in and make them want to learn more. Visit my intriguing website to experience the power of a single click that opens up unlimited possibilities.

Share your graphic easily on Pinterest to maximize its potential. Make a slideshow movie from your blog post or article to attract readers. You may easily create and distribute your material on YouTube with simple steps. Add a compelling video to your blog post smoothly. Our revolutionary function unleashes social media power! Strip engaging samples from your articles or posts and distribute them on Twitter with a compelling link to the complete material. Increase audience engagement and reach like never before. Try it now and see the magic!

Discover this extraordinary system's flawless operation. You can easily reach diverse audiences across platforms by cleverly reworking and recycling your great content. Maximize reach and effect by seamlessly distributing compelling formats on each platform. This fantastic solution unleashes your limitless potential.

Unleash Social Media Segmentation!

Instagram is a mesmerizing universe where every photo tells a story with many tags. Twitter is a mesmerizing world of trending tweets and hashtags. Discover the incredible value of these tags. Increase your internet presence with tags!

Our advanced content categorization function makes organizing and classifying information easy. Use tags to find captivating content—the power of our cutting-edge segmentation technology.

Chihuahua puppies with hashtags designed for cuteness seekers. These hashtags, carefully picked to capture the essence of these lovely critters, contrast with libertarian political content hashtags. Use hashtags to navigate social media with precision. Social media networks' powerful segmentation capabilities and features let you reach your intended audience easily.

Discover the truth: massive audiences with precise targeting are helpful. Discover the potential of social media marketing's advanced segmentation! This game-changing tool lets you effortlessly contact highly targeted audiences across various platforms. Skip wasted attempts and say hello to a fascinated audience who cares about what you say. Unlock the power of segmentation techniques to generate a highly refined and qualified audience. Enjoy higher revenues with this fantastic offer. With this novel strategy, you may significantly improve your deal-closing odds.

Discover the extraordinary power of automation for sharing captivating content across various platforms. You may easily share your views, tales, and thought-provoking ideas with a large audience with a few clicks. Enjoy the efficiency and convenience of automatic content sharing instead of manual sharing. Automation lets you reach more people, save time, and thrive on every platform.

Stop manually exploring Facebook or Twitter and copying and pasting text from documents. No more hours are spent carefully scheduling postings. These groundbreaking tools make social media management easy and efficient. Maximize productivity and efficiency through automation. Our cutting-edge platform lets you easily organize and publish up to six posts, freeing time for other vital duties. Use our advanced technologies to simplify your social media approach. Automate posting instead of manually posting. Feel the future of content management now.

Facebook lets you connect with friends and family like never before. Spend months exploring the colorful and dynamic community to discover unlimited possibilities. Imagine easily maintaining an active Facebook account and sharing engaging posts six to ten times daily or more. Best part? You won't have to monitor it continually since you've fed it lots of intriguing content.

Experience the utmost convenience with our cutting-edge automation technologies. Their capacity to seamlessly manage big feeds makes your tasks easier and more efficient. Abandon manual labor and embrace automation. Format your work easily in Excel to maximize its value. Convert it to CSV and plug it into these powerful tools easily. Remove the burden of manually entering materials and introduce a game-changing solution that boosts productivity and impact. Experience the unmatched benefit of saving time and effortlessly expanding your reach.

Discover how mailing lists can enable a dynamic two-track marketing strategy. This creative method can help you maximize your brand's potential and reach more people. Increase your marketing and watch your business grow. Take advantage of this chance to transform your marketing approach. Use email lists to achieve unprecedented achievement.

A highly focused email list can boost your content-based audience connection marketing campaign on social media. Captivate your audience with precision and refinement to find success. Your brand's message should resonate with those who matter most. Improve your marketing strategy with a well-crafted mailing list. Many assume they are going to greatness after carefully crafting their list.

Unleash your potential and start your millionaire adventure! The new, groundbreaking idea of being wonderfully unorthodox. It's not simply wrong—a bold declaration that challenges the revolutionary answer linking your existing procedure and ultimate success—the missing step! Unlock the secret to success with fantastic efficiency and effortless growth. Don't miss this vital item.

Discover the tremendous benefits of joining our exclusive email list. Enjoy the fantastic thrill of receiving a professionally curated selection of intriguing content suited to your interests and preferences. Join our acclaimed community today to discover unlimited possibilities. Welcome to a unique mailing list. Introducing "general," a fantastic discussion that covers every possible topic. Bringing a unique perspective. Conversations that exceed expectations. Explore undiscovered places with endless possibilities. I'm here to explore public interest using the topic's appeal. Discover the exciting puzzle of differentiating actual buyers from curious souls seeking knowledge as they journey to see if they can trust you.

The perfect sales strategy: start with a complete general list, then quickly transfer to the highly wanted buyer's list. Upsell and grow your business!

Discover the keys to outstanding achievement. Unleash your potential and achieve greatness. Experience our proven approaches' transforming impact. Allow yourself to excel and exceed expectations. Find the solution to your question and explore our exclusive general list of affordable gems—no matter the price, little issues. I understand your main goal is to let people quickly identify as purchasers. That's why I created a simple, hassle-free method that makes it easy for everyone. Discover the secret power of a dollar, an essential money that often goes overlooked in daily life.

Please find out how buying our product makes the pain disappear. A game-changing strategy: they are painlessly removed from your general list when they enter your buyer's list. A clean list of buyers remains. That list is a treasure trove, my friend. Discover the best platform for captivating your audience with intriguing case studies and convincing them to invest in your fantastic affiliate programs or exclusive products. Increase your buyer's list and achieve unprecedented success.

The groundbreaking two-track marketing campaign! Experience the unmatched power that has changed lives and created incredible fortune. My friend, avoid a common pitfall. Do not believe that having an extensive mailing list ensures success. The revolutionary new strategy that challenges the status quo. Experience a paradigm change like nothing before. Discover the transforming power of your following essential action.

Strategic multi-platform marketing gives your brand organic repetition. Having your brand flawlessly integrated across platforms will capture your target audience and leave an indelible mark. Unleash exponential growth when your brand message resonates across channels, strengthening its presence and connecting with customers. Take advantage of multi-platform marketing and see results.

Imagine having your social media accounts linked across all four leading platforms. Imagine a consistent symphony that gives you several chances to fascinate your listeners. Every post, update, and interaction can leave a mark. Embrace consistency to attract innumerable followers. Set the setting, ripen the apple, and capture the spotlight. Discover the truth: you do. Discover the thrilling possibilities when your brand engages fans on Facebook and quickly moves to Twitter.

Discover visual cohesion's strength! Brands with graphical solid resemblance have a fascinating presence across platforms. Imagine your audience seamlessly interacting and connecting with your brand throughout the internet.

A unique familiarity is built through time, resulting in unmatched comfort. This exceptional comfort may inspire them to join your distinguished email list when you make a persuasive call to action. Establish accounts on all the top platforms and experience organic development effortlessly. Watch success unfold as you start building your online presence. Creating a brand that effortlessly captures people's hearts everywhere they go. Passionate fans of your specialty love our unmatched appeal.

Discover the magic of content re-purposing and save money like never before. With this clever method, you can optimize the value of your existing material and boost your savings. Remove wasteful costs and replace them with a more cost-effective way to transform your organization.

Never underestimate content creation costs. Discover the power of forming a team of highly qualified, talented, professional, and experienced people from English-speaking countries. Even with such a large group, unexpected problems may develop.

Discover the opportunity to save thousands annually. Discover the appeal of talented writers from India, Pakistan, and the Philippines. They may be more affordable than American rates, but consider the cumulative impact on your spending.

Explore the limitless potential of social media marketing! Imagine the joy of creating intriguing material that can be recycled into many engaging formats. Let your imagination shine and maximize your brand's messaging across platforms. You can captivate, inspire, and make a lasting effect on your audience. Create content and see your brand's story unfold in ways you never thought possible. Experience massive expense reductions with this new solution.

Hire a talented Indian writer to unleash global brilliance. Just $1,000 per month can guarantee a steady stream of high-quality, customized content. Enjoy the ease and reliability of constant content production while focusing on business growth. Tap into Indian writers' vast potential to unlock endless possibilities. At this crucial point, you can invest $1,000 in the acclaimed individual's knowledge to uncover abundant, unmatched content. You can also cleverly turn their content into intriguing films, gorgeous infographics, or thought-provoking tweets. The options are endless!

Our diagram-making talents will make your ideas look great. I can also convert your carefully created videos' voice-overs into high-quality sound files. Behold the ability to make spectacular slideshows with these exceptional elements effortlessly. Repurpose your content to maximize its impact! Imagine the potential when format-specific platforms host your painstakingly created creations.

Start captivating your audience like never before. Make your content sparkle! Imagine effortlessly sharing your fascinating presentations with the globe. Your presentations will gain exposure and interaction using Slideshare's power. Showcase your ideas, thoughts, and expertise in a spectacular manner that will wow your audience. Slideshare lets you share your creativity. Pinterest enables you to share stunning infographics to unleash visual storytelling quickly.

Show your goods' magic on Instagram. Ensure the feed has gorgeous and intriguing general product photos that will leave you wanting more. Explore beauty and inspiration on Instagram with us. Enjoy the extraordinary and satisfy your senses. Let the magic begin today by following us. Twitter lets you easily share your questions with the world, maximizing their potential. Enjoy communicating with a large audience, starting interesting conversations, and discovering fresh ideas. Take advantage of social media to elevate your questions. Twitter awaits curiosity.

YouTube lets you share your videos with the world. Sharing your content in any format on Facebook, the world's most popular social media platform, is straightforward. Explore the fascinating mechanics of this clever invention. One strategic investment unlocks content optimization and boosts your internet presence. You may easily repurpose and distribute premium content, increasing your chances of garnering valuable visitors and awareness. Repurposed material can improve your digital success.

Discover continuous creation with our unique approach. Say goodbye to static ideas and hello to limitless, fascinating content. Adopt ongoing innovation and watch your brand flourish. The trick is creating captivating pieces that captivate viewers worldwide. Discover the best way to maximize their potential and value. A dramatic shift in content strategy: no more cranking out articles for a few glances. Explore the extraordinary. The one-way ticket to poverty!

Transform your content into attractive formats to maximize its potential. Distribute your material efficiently across platforms optimized for each design to maximize its potential. These eight persuasive reasons will fire your social media marketing game!

Fuel your excitement and success with these clear reasons. Take responsibility and conduct social media marketing right!

Discover how social media can transform customer feedback and engagement. Leverage dynamic channels that connect you directly to your audience to maximize brand potential. Social media can build a lively community where customers feel heard, respected, and involved. Use client input to improve your products and services and stay ahead of their requirements.

An innovative consumer feedback method! Stop waiting weeks or months for the organization to receive your critical thoughts. Our revolutionary company approach has changed client feedback and action. Real-time communication lets you see your thoughts' immediate impact. Join us on this exciting adventure as I connect customers and corporations to make your voice heard—and experience rapid response on social media. Discover the real power behind every like, share, remark, or retweet—your audience's feelings. Our unique real-time feedback method is the best tool for businesses to stay ahead! With this cutting-edge technology, you can adjust faster, answer concerns promptly, and open a world of creativity based on your audience's true desires. Stop guessing and start succeeding!

Social media also gives businesses an unmatched chance to engage with their customers. Authentic audience engagement unlocks power. From thoughtful responses to comments to fascinating live Q&A sessions, these meaningful interactions bring your brand to life and build trust. Engage with customers like never before. Our creative strategy builds brand loyalty and turns ordinary customers into brand advocates. See the fantastic impact as people enthusiastically promote your products and services.

Discover how social media may boost your website's SEO and organic visibility. Strategically use social media to promote your internet presence. Watch your website rank higher in search engines and grow naturally. Social media integration into your digital marketing plan unlocks unlimited opportunities for your brand. Don't

Discover the power of social media and its impact on SEO. Discover Google's game-changing power, which now prioritizes content that sparks social sharing and fascinating engagement. Social media can boost your content's potential. When your carefully prepared words are shared widely, they tell search engines that your material is valuable, reputable, and highly respected by users. Use this chance to make an impact and boost your internet visibility. Social sharing may make your content sparkle like never before.

Learn how a solid social media presence may quickly provide organic traffic to your website, increasing its visibility and rating. Content sharing unlocks your website's possibilities. Sharing valuable content creates a magical backlink, instantly enhancing your website authority. Enjoy watching your online visibility soar as your material becomes viral. Take advantage of this fantastic chance to boost your website's credibility and visibility. Let the world see how your content may increase your online success. Watch your website's search engine rating rise over time. However, by becoming a niche authority, you may engage and inspire your audience like never before.

For the next chapter, choose a social media marketing approach tailored to your internet business. I'll help you select a campaign that's effective and almost guaranteed to succeed. So buckle up for a voyage that will transform your internet profile! Join us at the place for excitement.

CHAPTER 3

Manage Social Media Marketing Campaigns Depending on Your Online Business

This chapter will captivate and test you. Prepare to focus on this chapter. The information may seem overwhelming, but it's vital to grasp. Discover why so many expert social media marketers fail. In other words, they're missing the boat by searching in the wrong area. This novel method of website and social media promotion is unique.

Let me show you the plan's apparent drawbacks. This eye-opening essay shows that the tried-and-true strategy fails in many areas, including social media marketing. Changing your perspective may help you perceive your project differently. Social media visitors are no longer the primary source. Step up your game and create plans for advertising each website or online business. Instead of a cookie-cutter approach, use your ingenuity to boost results.

Content is crucial to social media interactions. A cookie-cutter approach is only sometimes the best. Discover this absurd idea's massive scope. Preparing would be best since a content-based campaign exacerbates its negative consequences. Discover the truth: various businesses require different content and publishing strategies. Create and publish a masterpiece of social media content to match your website. Change, tweak, and personalize everything to create a seamless campaign your target audience will adore.

Excellent new website customizing possibilities are available. Discovering all the options will leave you spoiled for choice. A wealth of alternatives will inspire infinite investigation. Let your imagination go free to find your boundless possibilities. I differentiate publication, online retail (including drop shipping), email lists, and traffic sales websites here.

Discover the several business job possibilities. I'll simplify the endless options. I may divide the many businesses into four groups by looking at the ecosystem as a whole. Discover the intriguing details of these themes, each with its unique prerequisites. Focusing on certain qualities helps you achieve your goals. You may only get what you want if you think about it.

Social media marketers often fall into the trap of promoting blogs like drop shipping or e-commerce websites. Discover those that naturally convert social media followers into readers with intriguing content marketing. Check out how they balance selling and blogging like no one else. Their mastery of digital marketing will amaze you. This breakthrough answer will solve your issues overnight. Stop inefficient processes and encourage simplified operations. Learn about our groundbreaking idea that defies logic and challenges the status quo, made possible by cutting-edge technology. Expect to be surprised when you enter a world where common sense and the status quo are challenged. Enjoy solving riddles while exploring the mystery.

Discover that different methods require different materials. The first and most crucial step of your online marketing plan is developing and emphasizing your digital entity's unique value proposition—secrets to blog marketing success. Dive into our information ocean to find enlightenment. Discover the riches in our digital refuge, where the words you read will captivate your curious mind as they dance across the screen.

A vast material repository can satisfy your interest. Explore the power of collaborative invention as diverse individuals create captivating new content. Welcome to your publishing platform, where your words may reach readers worldwide. Our cutting-edge technology makes telling storytelling easy. Create a literary legacy and join the renowned. Do you have the courage to start a business? Stop searching—I have everything you need to create a successful dropshipping business. Please browse our vast selection of excellent items and order quickly. Stop waiting and leverage Shopify's full potential to join the thriving e-commerce community. Oberlo offers hundreds of high-quality Aliexpress goods.

Try our cutting-edge e-commerce platform to see how easy and profitable it is. Customers may order items with a few clicks, and our advanced technology will handle Aliexpress shipping. Best of all, you keep what's left! Use our easy and practical way to maximize revenues. Large retailers or one-person shops can use us. Congratulations on opening an online store! When your internet business is successful, you may reach customers worldwide. Display your beautiful products and offer a top-notch shopping experience with a few mouse clicks.

Our innovative publishing firm will permanently revolutionize your book view. Learn the stark difference between social media marketing and mailing lists to optimize income. Compare the practical approaches for your significant mailing list to those for your internet business. Watch concentrated marketing improve your business and yield extraordinary returns. Discover the benefits of customizing your content. Try a personalized technique and see what happens. Integrating all your information with your unique ways will change your life. When combined, these two forces provide limitless possibilities. Accept several methods and discover your excellent resource selection. Browse our various selections, carefully selected to match your needs. Try anything in our extensive collection. I have everything from high-tech devices to luxury couture.

After inspiring you to think imaginatively about the fantastic individuals who visit your website, let me show you the many intriguing content types you may use. Break free from mental constraints and experiment. Creative thinkers have the world at their fingertips. Learn how to use your various tools to produce unique content.

I am happy to provide our cutting-edge solution tailored to your organization. A vast selection of content types to boost your websites! Every kind of content has some appeal, but to create an effect, you need to specialize. Prepare for a thrilling advertising journey!

Audio clips—exciting new media! Our fantastic assortment will take you to music and sound, from moving songs to Slideshows—an intriguing new media. Enjoy a breathtaking visual experience.

Introduce you to infographics, an excellent medium. These stunning masterpieces are the perfect blend of some of our innovative diagrams! These artworks will amaze and enlighten.

This is the most comprehensive list of intriguing blog links that will take you somewhere fresh and thrilling every time you click. Introduce you to video, an excellent medium. A visual feast will transport you.

Links that go beyond mental connections change everything!

Seeing so many excellent social media marketers focus solely on link promotion, I feel sad and uneasy. Discover their ideal culmination. Absolutely! Links are essential for online presence. Put yourself in their shoes to understand their values and views. By imagining others' perspectives, we can obtain knowledge and compassion that can be utilized to bridge gaps and form friendships. Empathizing helps us appreciate our shared humanity and our distinctions.

One mouse click unleashes instant traffic. Diversifying content helps you develop a more substantial brand presence on your target site.

Audio, visuals, and graphs may persuade in many scenarios. Why use plain links when you can engage users with captivating content? In a world where we receive many links daily, standing out and providing information more engagingly and memorably is crucial. Success awaits those who keep their promises. To attract your target audience, use engaging content types. Contacting them personally will increase the likelihood of them clicking on your link.

Discover the sad fact that many get this wrong. Understand content strategy. Start with connections, then add different content kinds for engagement. Impress your audience by using all your skills. They know they're a day late and a dollar short. Discover the various benefits of avoiding certain activities. Discover derivative material's advantages. Putting it front and center hooks listeners immediately. Use natural links to create an intriguing tale. Your site's theme should guide your layout. A non-customized format won't meet your needs.

Develop a competitive edge by researching their intriguing world. Explore your competitors' domains and pay attention to their exciting content. Learn about their perfect presentation. Their kind gift of picture quotes opens up new inspiration and visual enjoyment. Take a deep breath and prepare for a visual and linguistic feast that inspires and uplifts you with each page. Their profound teachings and skillful delivery will motivate you. Find out the love diagrams. I provide a selection that defies chance. Learn everything you need to engage ideal consumers. The secret methods for contacting your target audience are disclosed.

Now is the time for daring, out-of-this-world ideas. This novel solution will revolutionize the game. I'll disclose a groundbreaking innovation that will wow you. Forget your problems and look forward to a bright future. This attempt is unique; it's a chance to understand why your competitors could be more active in adopting a comparable technique. Now is the moment to study others' ways. Decoding their shapes gives you a strategic advantage and new insights.

Giving your organization a unique identity may help you maximize its potential. Options expand significantly after this. Try several formats and approaches to discover the perfect fit for your firm.

Discover success via reverse engineering. Study your profession's early adopters' tactics. Only then will you be ready for the challenges ahead. Give your tasks to specialists to attain academic success without worry. Enjoy the simplicity of having consummate specialists execute your work. Use this opportunity to save time and improve results. Let them do your homework, and your academic experience will improve.

Recognize your numerous achievements and use them to achieve more. Allow your forward momentum to take you higher. Recognizing and developing your skills will provide you with endless possibilities. Keep up the excellent work, and you will amaze yourself. Find their hidden value and give an enticing offer to keep them wanting more. Find out if watching for what others miss works. Discover how to reach your potential and leave unfulfilling activities. Take an action that boosts your progress. Stop your money-losing initiatives and start a bright future.

Discover your answers. Make sure your carefully crafted content matches your company's needs. Your sharing techniques should also reflect your brand's attitude. Make reverse engineering transformative and discover its endless potential. Learn to comprehend complexities and find the fantastic journey ahead. Discover how even a little reverse engineering may boost your career. You can own the world if you work hard enough at reverse engineering.

CHAPTER 4

The Classic Way to Do Social Media Marketing and Why it is a Waste of Your Time

This session should start with a discussion of other social media marketers. Imagine seeing a handful of pennies on the ground and resisting the urge to pick them up.

However, it will knock you off balance. It will make you feel like you're receiving something when you're not, and you'll give in to your darkest desires.

Since humans choose the easiest choice, this is usual. They're hard to blame. However, telling you what happens will help you learn from your error and focus on doing things right.

Traditional Social Media Advertising Methods

How would one usually promote on social media? It's easy to find out. You should only "follow," "like," or "friend" those interested in your specialization on Instagram, Twitter, or Facebook.

After following several individuals, many may follow back. Only 20%–30% of 100 Twitter followers will follow you back.

This is when things become worse. Traditional social media marketers spam fans and friends. They'd bombard you with unrelated content and unfollow you. See the trend? Send likes, spam, and unfollow. I'd argue it's random, but "professional marketers" use many intricate systems to attain their goals.

This procedure was perfect till recently. Many Twitter users were drawn to this tactic. But no longer. This practice can get you banned from the service.

If you get traffic this way, it won't be good. Why? Targeting is impossible. No screening is done on your potential followers.

You started following them, so they followed. Shopping variety—where is it? Where will they shoot? The numbers game of speculating won't get you anywhere. No amount of effort pays off.

You may succeed with this selling strategy. That's not my point. My point is that opportunity, time, and effort expenses aren't worth the advantages. Quality work will benefit you.

People Desire Quality.

Social Media Marketing Revolution's success depends on helpful content. Work will speak for itself. Your content will pre-sell your brand. What you post online represents you. It represents the firm values you want people to associate with it.

The Sad Reality

The rules have changed, so "follow, get followed, spam, and unfollow" is still thriving for specific individuals but is usually frowned upon. Social media interactions determine excellent and negative feedback. Take Facebook as an example. Facebook used to have huge traffic potential—no more.

Keeping a huge Facebook following demands frequent involvement. With usual participation rates, success is anticipated. That's how bad things are. Therefore, I'm explaining why "classic social media marketing" is obsolete.

Variations That Failed

It would be improper for me not to tell you about failed social media marketing attempts. First off, hashtag searching is worthless. Marketers search for trending hashtags. They would post niche content with irrelevant hashtags.

This lets them "hitch a ride" on hashtag popularity. They know certain hashtags attract specific users. They're attempting to steal hashtag trend enthusiasts' attention.

Low-quality visits are inevitable. If your content is unrelated to consumers' wants, they won't click through. Even worse, someone may report you.

Influencer spamming has failed before and should be avoided. There are prominent persons in almost every industry. Watch this on Facebook or Twitter. Many niche Facebook and Twitter groups exist.

Regularly quoting these influencers in your work is only worthwhile if it provides value. Having a good reason to communicate with opinion leaders would be best. Getting their attention is only the start. Promoting your product only because you like it is a poor idea.

Your engagement label should emphasize what they did. If an influencer talked about the latest sports footwear fashions, I might utilize it to create a piece about how they affect large shoe and apparel manufacturers' profits.

I exclusively connect to high-quality, relevant stuff, so this influencer will be very interested in what I say. Do you get the nuances? Do you see my connection? I relate this to a foreign exchange influencer when talking about Bitcoin.

The person will get upset. Do you see the difference? Automatic publishing with marketing will succeed. You throw spaghetti against the wall and hope to get some sticks. If you schedule posts on Twitter, Facebook, Pinterest, etc., it's impossible to predict how many people will interact with them. It would be best if you grabbed readers' attention. Promote your social media profiles to qualified, established audiences.

Maximize your best work. If done well, automated social media posting may be beneficial. The shotgun approach to social media marketing may provide the same disappointing results as other marketers.

CHAPTER 5

Steps to Quicker and Easier Modern SM Marketing

In this chapter, I'll provide a high-level summary of the training's 10 Steps. This methodology is the result of several unsuccessful attempts. You may rest assured that I have heard of any "hot" or "groundbreaking" social media marketing techniques or strategies you may have encountered. That is something I have accomplished. This education is the total of our life's experiences.

What does not work, I also know. I'm aware that everyone's knowledge base, availability, and budget for a given job are unique. I am aware of the constraints. I can relate to the general public's skepticism about social media advertising. As a result, I developed a 10-step Program that social media marketers of various experience and financial levels can follow.

You can put this social media marketing strategy up to mostly run itself, making it one of the most effective options available. I'm about to outline the steps, so please understand me. Steps. Observing them is mandatory. There is no way around this. Just because I've used specific terms or am discussing general concepts doesn't mean you already know everything there is to know.

Please read this as a beginner learning social media marketing for the first time. Don't be shocked if the strategy I'm teaching you doesn't pan out if you don't have that attitude and are willing to skip stages. What gives? You breezed right past it. You were in a hurry. There were important details that you glossed over.

You'll need to take things slowly and carefully to get the most out of this software. Continuing only once you've mastered the current phase would be best. You probably need more time, but please do this properly. If you don't put forth the effort, you have only yourself to blame if things go wrong. So, do I have this straight? Okay.

For more efficient and effective social media marketing, consider these ten steps.

1. Finding and targeting specific niches
2. Methods of Organizing Existing Content
3. Competitors' best material can be reverse-engineered.
4. Develop optimized data for the payload
5. Effectively promoting your mailing list.
6. Explore the potential of cross-platform content repurposing

7. Optimized content distribution

8. Raising the Stakes of Targeting

9. Modify your approach to list sales.

10. Spend wisely what you've earned.

In total, there are ten measures. I know these sound simple. They look simple, but the devil is in the details.

CHAPTER 6

Niche Research and Targeting it the Right Way

Whenever I meet a social media marketer, they ask me how to increase traffic. Build up any old site and stop worrying about specialty research and consumer intelligence.

Let's cut to the chase and get to the "good stuff." That's the thinking I encounter frequently, and it's one of the main reasons so many people fail in this game.

Put it bluntly, you'll be chasing your tail until you figure out which tree you should be barking up. I apologize if I keep comparing things to dogs. These are the best. Most individuals are futilely squandering their time and energy on activities that contribute little to their bottom line.

Many of these, and probably all of them, may be easily avoided with little preliminary niche targeting. In other words, focus on your target market. Now that you have a detailed description of your ideal customer, you can set out to locate them on various social networking sites.

It may seem wild, and it certainly does sound odd. Still, people on social media sites are already discussing or displaying interest in whatever you promote, no matter how esoteric, obscure, or bizarre. As a marketer, you are responsible for identifying potential customers on these sites.

The first step is zero in on somebody you want to buy from your company. Unfortunately, very few marketers pay any attention to this. Social media marketing is seen as little more than a traffic generation exercise by these people. There you have it. That's what you're supposed to do. That settles the matter, period. Knowing exactly who you're writing for is crucial to your success.

This is only sometimes simple. Sometimes, you feel that "educated guesses" regarding your target audience are the best option. That fails to function in the vast majority of cases. Fortunately, there's a more straightforward method. The more time and resources you waste taking wild assumptions and shooting in the dark, the more you lose.

The problem may be solved quickly if you locate your rivals. Seriously. Locate them, please. And believe me, there will always be at least one rival on social media, no matter how obscure, obscure, or "unknown" your specialty may seem.

Find that company and hire them to undertake market and niche analysis. Look at your rivals' social media pages to see how they communicate with your target demographic.

Find out who they are pursuing by using deduction. Watch out for the people they intend to hurt. Check out how they divide themselves up. Said, focus on the hashtags that accompany their posts.

These hints should be sufficient to get you started. You'll have a head start this way. You aren't helpless and without any idea what to do. You can access some objective data that has been tried and tested instead.

Find Your Niche Market

Every company may be seen from one of two angles, and you must keep that in mind as you strategize. The wider your target audience, the more approaches you may use. Various specialty subsets are available for investigation.

You need to know how this operates because even if you think you have a well-defined niche, there are likely multiple sub-niches within that larger one. Possible distinct subsegments exist there.

You should know exactly what your specialty is, as well as the smaller niches that exist inside it. Once again, you can try reverse engineering your rivals' systems. Whatever the case may be, you must act now. This is the knowledge that you must get.

You may now visit YouTube, Facebook, Twitter, and Pinterest to find your niche market. Now, look at the size of the material and messaging spaces available on various sites, such as Facebook pages, groups, Google Plus communities, Twitter hashtags, Pinterest Pinboards, and current YouTube channels.

Check out these venues to determine if there is a sizable audience for your specialty. A red flag should go up if the material on a given platform isn't very relevant to your thing. There needs to be more interest. It may not be worthwhile due to the small amount of the audience.

On the other hand, you can see it as a good indication if you discover that other movies cover the same ground as your own. However, you will need to dig deeper into this issue. Think about how many rivals you have in your market.

There will be trouble if there appear to be many rivals vying for the same market share. If, however, you find that there is a great deal of information aimed at your niche but that a small number of sources create it, take this as a positive indicator.

Think about how engaged your intended viewers are. Take a look at the stuff that's being discussed about your specific field. How active is the community? Do folks talk about this stuff? Is the # trendy?

Please keep an eye out for these and other measures of effectiveness. Suppose you can make sense of these signals. In that case, you'll know with absolute certainty whether or not a particular platform is suitable for promoting your niche's interests or whether you should go elsewhere.

Specifics of Your Target Market:

Observing how your specialty is represented on other sites is essential for reverse engineering. Hashtags, classes, keywords, labels, and tagging schemes all fall within this category. Put them to use in the analysis I just outlined. Sub-niches exist in every market. Therefore, you'll want to create a sub-niche or unique selling proposition for your content to avoid being overwhelmed by the competition.

You're still capitalizing on a huge market, but you aren't dooming yourself by going up against established industry players. You will likely need to try a few until you locate a promising niche.

CHAPTER 7

Your Secret Social Media Marketing Weapon: Content Curation

Finding content is the next stage after deciding on a certain sub-niche to target and completing in-depth research into the social media platforms frequented by members of that sub-niche or niche segment.

There's good news and terrible news here. The good news is that you may expect significant financial savings. Unfortunately, you'll have to devote significantly more time and focus. There is just no denying it. You must maintain a high standard regarding the material you want to post on social media.

Your brand should be strengthened with every piece of content you publish. This is not up for discussion. You can't just pick stuff that relates to your niche.

That won't attract the correct kind of customers. It would be best if you had more than that to build the trust and authority required to turn the targeted, high-quality social media traffic you're getting into actual dollars.

A Definition of Content Curation.

I've already explained why content curating is so financially advantageous. You aren't going to use your original work, after all. Sharing the work of others on your social media profiles is what "content curation" is all about. As a result, everyone benefits.

You're effectively giving the content's creator free promotion by spreading links and summaries. Conversely, you increase your credibility by providing your followers highly targeted, specialized, value-added material in exchange for their attention.

There are triumphs for all those involved. Everyone, including the user, yourself, and the original content producer, benefits from this situation. This is how things are meant to operate. You win big since you don't have to spend nearly as much time or money creating brand-new material, giving you a significant financial advantage.

Writing your material or hiring a company in the United States or elsewhere to do it for you may rapidly become costly.

Curating content is a low-cost strategy for establishing your expertise in the eyes of your target audience. You are using someone else's work. You'll be able to win their trust while also entertaining them. Time is an issue here. Although you won't shell out any cash, you will invest some time.

As I've already indicated, being picky is essential in content curation. If consumers discover that you only curate and disseminate low-quality information that could be related to your niche, any goodwill you've built up for your brand will quickly evaporate. That won't do the trick. Not.

Use Effective Content Curation Techniques

Now that you know where your target audience spends their time online, you can boost your reputation by sharing material from reputable, authoritative sources on the social media channels where they spend the most time.

You'll be interspersing those resources with your unique posts. Incentives for subscribing to your mailing list are something you'll periodically remind your audience to check out. This is the proper strategy for winning.

If people follow you, they should expect nothing but the best from you. Whether or not you had a hand in creating that content, your followers will benefit from following your account anyway.

Specialized content is provided for them. You can earn their confidence over time by consistently providing people with high-quality content. They begin focusing on the content you've provided. People start paying attention to the materials you distribute, which motivates them to join your mailing list.

That's a crucial part. You add in some of your creative flair here and there. You establish a positive reputation by only delivering the material from third parties. You then combine this with your unique material on par with the rest of your transmission. When they've warmed up to your brand, they'll be ready to engage with your call-to-action material.

You encourage people to take advantage of the goodies you're offering. Whether your freebie is software, a brochure, discount vouchers, or a full-fledged book doesn't matter. You act unethically by asking for their email addresses in exchange for the reward. That's how you get people to sign up for your newsletter.

In addition, you encourage people who sign up for your mailing list to forward the messages you give them. You could ask them to share the email with their contacts. Perhaps you'd like it if they copied and pasted the content into their Facebook wall.

What I Like Most

One of content curation's finest features is how easily it can be automated. Seriously. This strategy for content marketing lends itself well to robotic execution. It's as simple as collecting the links to the external sources you're using in an Excel spreadsheet. Then, you change the

Create a comma-separated values (CSV) file that can be read by scheduling apps like Hootsuite and SocialOomph.

You won't need to key in every detail by hand. Planning doesn't have to be done manually. All of this is automatable in software. That's fantastic, right? You may boost your reputation while doing less actual labor. With that in mind, you must prioritize the quality of your content.

Paying Close Attention to Details Is Crucial

It would be best to fight the urge to acquire everything remotely connected to your specialty that comes up in simple keyword searches on Google or social media networks. That's a sure way to ruin your reputation. As a result of your efforts, your social

Watching your hard work and dedication to building your media brand go up in smoke would be terrible since the quality of the stuff you're collecting might vary considerably.

There might be stretches when you send nothing but the most insightful updates about your specialty, followed by periods where you send nothing but fluff. If you were a potential fan, what would you think? They may see your company as unprofessional or untrustworthy. Whatever the situation may be, you won't succeed in persuading consumers that your brand is dedicated to excellence.

Selecting material requires careful consideration. The items must be read in their entirety. Make sure it's fresh, up-to-date, and written effectively. Of course, this will take some time. The benefit is apparent: reduced financial outlay.

The material you provide is a reflection of your company. Therefore, it's vital to choose it carefully. Its quality will either elevate or diminish your company's reputation. Your option is open.

CHAPTER 8

Reverse Engineer Your Competitors' Top Content

I recommended incorporating some of your unique material into the mix in the last chapter. The question on your mind is, presumably, "How do I know which content to produce?"

I've already highlighted two approaches to this during the training. You may let your competitors do your homework for you by figuring things out on their own and engaging in various experiments, or you can try to figure things out on your own and engage in multiple experiments.

I trust you now see the most straightforward way forward. That goes without saying. Your original material ought to be just as good, if not better, than the content you are putting out. They won't bite if your followers suspect you're trying to trick them. You may need to remember they trust your company.

They like that you're keeping track of all this data and will likely continue monitoring your social media profiles, but you should expect more from them. They have no reason to sign up for your email list.

For what reason should they? The quality of your writing could be better. If they look at the quality of the third-party content you share and compare it to the unique content you make, they will immediately identify your flaws. Can you see where I'm going wrong?

If you want people to take your brand seriously, you need to put out quality material. Thankfully, it's simpler than you may have imagined. Just study how they did things backward.

Check out what has sold the best for them. How do you know that? Examine the content's social media metrics. How many "likes" do their best pieces typically receive? Is there a count for the number of "shares?" Is there anything else that may indicate this material's popularity?

Check out how many people have commented on the article. A backlink checker may determine how many other blogs or websites link to a particular content.

This is how you evaluate the overall efficacy of any piece of material before adopting it as a "template" for your work. I'm not advocating theft, but rather that you take what works and build upon it to create something even more significant.

It's important to zero down on successful strategies. By analyzing the most shared articles produced by your rivals, you may create content that is more likely to be successful. They're popular among the people you want to reach. You won't be throwing away time or resources speculating.

One of the most typical blunders made by those working in social media marketing. They fancy themselves experts in their field and think they know what will be "hot" regarding content. They produce a wide variety of works they consider to be outstanding but which ultimately fail to impress.

If you were to create a hundred pieces of that kind of original material, just ten would get any momentum at all in your area. It wastes too much money and time. Fortunately, there's a more effective strategy. The key is determining what makes your rivals' most popular content click.

Put that to use as a jumping-off point. You may tweak them and make your changes, or use them as-is to get a head start on something new. When you first get started, at least you're in the general vicinity. You aren't only stumbling about in the dark.

Study Your Victories

Monitor your analytics after you have begun curating and incorporating your unique material. The most popular pieces of your fabric should be highlighted for you.

You should pay special attention to the curated third-party material that generates the most retweets, Facebook shares, or other forms of social media interaction.

They touched a raw nerve on some level. They were a big hit with the people in the crowd. Seek out these well-received collections and develop your takes on them.

Similarly, a tiny fraction will be widely read and shared even if you produce a large quantity of unique material. Take note of those. Find it. When you've found a winning formula, replicate it. Maintain coherence and consistency in your approach to related topics and material.

The trick is to build on what is already successful. Get rid of the useless items. Focus on what you do well. Make New Versions of Your Best Content on Different Platforms

Now that you know what works in content, stop trying to figure it out yourself. It would be best to keep doing it, but you must also shift your focus elsewhere. Make a fork or a port to another system.

Take social media as an example: a certain kind of blog post does well everywhere. Determine its primary ideas and recurring patterns, then use that information to inspire a new blog entry. Find out if that helps.

You'll be onto something good if you can replicate that degree of success. This is not a random occurrence. This won't be a one-and-done occurrence. You've hit on something that resonates with the listeners.

Taking it to the next level is the next step. Make videos instead of merely writing about the topic on your site. Construct specialized charts. Develop some infographics.

Use the social media sites that cater to these media to disseminate these materials. You may use social media like Twitter and Facebook to spread links to your articles. Use YouTube to share your video content. Pinterest is the place to publish your diagrams and infographics.

Digging deeper, look at your most popular blog pieces and extract the most crucial questions to utilize as tweet prompts. Send out many tweets with the same message over a week. Drop them gradually rather than all at once. But if you ask the appropriate questions, you may get attention on Twitter. Use relevant hashtags with these.

The benefits of content curation include cost savings and an improved ability to focus on what you do best. You zero down on the working aspects and figure them out so that you can consistently crank out winning material.

This, of course, will not occur instantly. You must keep trying new things until you identify the topics that consistently resonate with your target demographic.

CHAPTER 9

Fine Tune Your Payload Content

As I've already indicated, the social signals of the excellent third-party materials you're collecting may serve as inspiration for your original content. When you go through your sources, you will repeatedly come across specific types of information that generate significant online discussion.

The objective signs indicate this material is of excellent quality and in high demand. You'll then be able to create your unique take on the material.

It can serve as a model for your work. One alternative is to start with a round of curation. You may set your social media accounts to post third-party material of a high standard automatically and with strong social signals.

The curating campaign lasts for a few weeks. You'll start to see a trend very quickly. Eventually, you'll notice that certain pieces of content receive significantly more attention than others. After that, you're free to create your variation.

Both strategies are used in the content selection process. The first option is what I do if I need folks to join my email list quickly. However, I'll continue with the second approach if I need to learn more about the niche or my target audience. There needs to be a correct response. It's easier to say without knowing further details.

The second approach is preferable since it allows you to tailor your unique content strategy to the performance of your social media profiles. It's important to remember that even if third-party information of high quality may contain many objective social signals, such signals may have been developed in various settings.

The first publisher did something you need to do. See how it benefits you? Still, if time is of the essence, the first approach is perfectly viable. However, the second approach is worthwhile if you have the time. Please start with the curation, give it time to run, and then look at the data. It would be best if you noticed a trend.

Popular content is typically concentrated around a few central ideas. Almost all of the content that did well on the internet for several of my campaigns revolved around a single question. That's how niche the requirements of your target audience might be.

Look at the content's click-through rate and engagement to see how well it's doing. This is where many social media marketers need help. They mistakenly believe that interaction is the critical factor. The value of engagement signals, such as the number of likes, shares, and comments, is negligible if readers don't go on to engage with the content by clicking through.

Keep in mind that, in the end, what you need is traffic. That's the whole point of all this effort on your part. It will do you no favor to avoid getting preoccupied with the number of retweets, likes, or comments your content receives. Click-through rates require constant monitoring.

There must be a connection between interest and action rate. You should pay greater attention to information if its click-through rate is high.

Pay Special Attention to Content That Gets Lots of Clicks and Engagement

After finding successful pieces of curated material, the next step is to examine them in great detail. Think about the issues that would be of interest to your target audience. Do they try to evoke feelings with the headline? Do they include question marks in the subheadings? Do they force the individual to follow along or present everything front and center?

Take care with the superficial details. People do indeed evaluate a book by its cover, which is valid with blog postings and articles. In what kind of format do these resources come? Do they have a broad vision? Do the pages have images in the header? Do they employ schematics? Precisely, what are they doing, you ask?

After you've thought through and settled on answers to all of these questions, you may go on to develop your content specification document. Use this as a model for your work.

Now check that you are relying on only some viral articles. It's possible that unexpected success with third-party material was just a fluke. That piece of fabric went viral for whatever reason, and the firm behind it could be lucky. That won't do you any good.

The success of several pieces of curated content should serve as a basis for your template. In this approach, you can rest assured that you will get some respectable outcomes even if you partially meet all the requirements.

Make Up Some Content for the Payload Based on the Above

Now that you have your outline, you can focus on developing unique content to attract and retain readers. You'll use this material to get individuals to sign up for your mailing list. They should avoid this, having gotten eager to sign up for your email list. This is the type of material that is most likely to be believed and spread.

How enthused are you? Do not get your hopes up, though. Many folks go in but sabotage themselves because the material they write for the payload reads like advertising. That's just blatant spam. That's not something anyone would entrust to you.

You're just attempting to play games and pull tricks. No way could work. Instead, the material should be helpful, like an informational commercial. You have a product to sell, but the value your customers receive must be substantial.

You have to balance on the edge of a cliff. There's a fine line between forcing information down people's throats and helping them out at no cost to yourself. A reasonable middle ground between the two is what you need to find.

Ultimately, it's all about ensuring the stuff you put out is valuable. Your content needs to be helpful to the individuals who read it. That's the way to establish trustworthiness. That's the way to get folks interested in signing up for your mailing list.

Remember that your list is meant to improve their daily life somehow. If the information you provide has no value, you will have difficulty making that impact. I'm hoping it's clear to you.

CHAPTER 10

Market Your List Right

After deciding on the material to be sent in the "payload," the following step is determining the kind of freebie necessary to get readers to join the mailing list.

The best-case scenario is that others recognize your worth. All they have to do is look at the material you publish and the critical insights they gain from your premium content. They get a taste of who you are and what you offer with this premium material and understand why it would benefit them to join your mailing list.

Things don't pan out like that, though. People still need encouragement to join your mailing list, even if you have the finest blog entries and articles on the web. Incentives play a crucial role in this regard.

You'll repackage pricey stuff that people would enjoy, but you'll make it available for free. You wrote a book on it, or you could create a reference guide, condense it into a pamphlet, or program it.

Whatever the situation, offering such valuable information for free will encourage individuals to sign up for your mailing list. In return, they receive a free copy of the offer for their email address.

A bribe of morality, if you will. You're using incentives to get individuals to join your mailing list. They typically wouldn't do it. The quality of your blog posts and articles makes no difference; very few people will bother to join your list. That's the way things are.

Determining an Appropriate Motivator

You'll agree that providing freebies in exchange for email addresses makes sense if you want to grow your mailing list. Often, people only need a little bit of encouragement. The average person requires a little sugar on the happening deal. They need an incentive to finally commit to joining your mailing list.

The next step is to decide what type of freebie you'll provide in exchange for email addresses. The good news is that you won't be starting from square one—no need to speculate wildly.

You may avoid blind fire by preparing correctly. If you analyze your best-performing original material, you should have all you need to create an attractive bonus.

Suppose you operate a gardening blog and find that your readers are particularly interested in articles on tomatoes (as seen by clicking the "share" button and other forms of engagement). In that case, consider offering a free book on constructing a low-cost greenhouse for growing tomatoes as a giveaway. See how it benefits you?

Focus on the unique material that is performing the best. Please look at the questions they address and those they don't. This way, you may leverage your most shared articles as a springboard for incentive-based articles.

You tell your readers that there's more information available at this link if they want it, which they probably do because the material they're now perusing is incomplete. Your "squeeze page" may be found at that URL. The squeeze page promotes your freebie and explains why people should download it. The process is simple. All you're doing is selling access to the same premium content that links to your free stuff.

Since they do not provide such information, they direct readers elsewhere. They do admirably in establishing trustworthiness and authority. They do an excellent job of improving your readers' lives, but it's clear that they need certain information. They need to sign up to receive the supplementary resources. It doesn't cost you a dime. They won't be out any money, but they must join your mailing list.

This is the proper procedure for creating a mailing list. It needs to be well integrated with your paid material. It's not a good idea to come up with incentives or freebies that have nothing to do with the work you're doing at the moment. There is a high probability that you will fail. Adding value to your disseminating content is as simple as generating relevant incentive content. A sense of seclusion is also present.

Once your audience knows who you are and what your brand stands for, thanks to your content, you can offer them a bonus. People unfamiliar with your brand must be aware of this limited-time offer.

Always prioritize growing your mailing list in the content you create from scratch. Please emphasize the email list's importance before highlighting the incentive material's worth. This may seem backward, but if you stop to consider that they are subscribing to a mailing list, then it makes perfect sense.

You're trying to entice them with the gift you're offering. Nothing more than an email address entry field is intended. Utilize your unique material to promote the idea that readers can access this supplementary material. You shouldn't be surprised if they sign up for your list only to immediately unsubscribe when they realize they don't care about it.

You're in a precarious position once again. One goal is to generate interest in the freebie you're offering in return for an email address. In contrast, you want potential subscribers to appreciate why they should join your mailing list.

This is the correct strategy. Your email list should be prioritized in all of your unique material. Your original material should emphasize that people who join your mailing list will continue to acquire relevant information from you even after receiving the incentive.

People are less likely to sign up for your mailing list only to quickly unsubscribe when you promote it with material that has shown to be successful in the past. They appreciate the benefits the list may provide in their daily lives.

Then, you promote the access to premium features that members receive. It's a bonus, to put it another way. The item is secondary on the list. Please keep the list consistent with the incentives individuals receive for signing up for it.

You want to highlight the list first, so this is apparent. Still, the premium material (whether it's a free book, booklet, cheat sheet, pre-recorded video, or anything else) must be presented to incentivize visitors to purchase.

That's what it comes down to. Aside from the incentive, all of your unique material and, by implication, your website should encourage the viewer to realize the value of becoming a list member.

Many people who work in social media marketing need to realize this. They believe the key to success is in effectively advertising the reward. What happens, for instance, once you've convinced them to sign up for your list in return for the greenhouse guide? Nothing, you read it correctly.

Why? You made such a big deal out of the greenhouse guide that individuals signed up for the mailing list without knowing what they were getting in return. It's common for some of your subscribers to report your updates as spam.

Because they were preoccupied with acquiring the free book, they were surprised to find correspondence from your mailing list. Miscommunication on your website or blog causes this problem frequently.

You can't afford to act like this in the game. It was a concerted effort on your part to attract so many people from social media. You put in a lot of work and money to make your brand reputable. You need to include the target in promoting your email list.

The list must be sold before the incentive may be utilized to motivate buyers. This is the proper order of importance. Nothing else will work.

Maximize Your Squeeze Page's Shareability.

I've already emphasized how important it is to promote your email list through your content. Your squeeze page's content should be used to make additional sales pitches. However, well-designed squeeze pages are acceptable. That won't do the trick. Your squeeze page's design is crucial. After all, you've landed on a dedicated employment website.

You need to convince visitors of this page to sign up for your mailing list for reasons other than the reward. Although the incentive is the main focus of a squeeze page, you still need to make it apparent that visitors are signing up for your mailing list.

That being said, argue your point. For what possible reason should we follow your updates? Just what are the benefits of remaining on your email list? What use would it provide them?

Remember that "What's in it for me?" is continuously being asked. Your squeeze page has to provide a solid and convincing answer to that query. Your squeeze page's design has to be conducive to making that connection, and it also needs to be social media marketing friendly.

Your squeeze page might benefit from a Pinterest-friendly image. Consider including a YouTube-friendly video on your squeeze page.

The possibilities are practically endless. Your squeeze page must be optimized for sharing on social networks. Additionally, it needs to be effective in bringing in new employees.

Create an Appropriate Verification Page

Welcome new subscribers and thank them for joining your list. You must also forewarn them of the nature of the information they will get. Convince them that what they did was the appropriate thing to do. Please give them the impression that they've accomplished something great. In addition to obtaining the digital freebie you're offering, they'll be provided with helpful knowledge on a topic they're struggling with.

The list can be sold in this manner. To turn social media visitors into buyers, you need more than just a lot of hype and promotion of the premium. No way is it going to happen. The list needs to be sold. Having faith in the list is essential.

CHAPTER 11

Unlock the Power of Repurposed Content

I covered this in greater detail in an earlier chapter, but it bears repeating because of its significance. When you write anything new for your blog or website, you do it with the knowledge that your target audience will well receive it. You are aware of the high demand for this subject matter.

Not only are you selecting material based on your data, but you're also basing your selection on the social signals of your competitor's content, which you reverse-engineered. In other words, you're basing your work on successfully used information.

You aren't just making educated guesses and holding your breath, hoping that anything works. You have instead created a judgment based on what is practical. Congratulations. But it would be best if you did more than that. Once you see that this material is performing well in terms of clicks and social media interaction, the next step is to repurpose it for other uses. Transform them into new content and distribute them again on sites catering to those new forms.

If you see that a particular blog article generates many shares and hits, you could find it helpful to reformat it into a series of questions. This is easy to do because, at its core, all material is just questions and their answers. Though the information may not directly answer the reader's inquiries, it is designed to address their problems even if they are not immediately apparent. Questions might be posed in response to these worries.

Reduce your most impactful and successful content to a sequence of questions. Then, the article or blog post that addresses each query is linked. Combine these tweets with relevant hashtags to reach your target audience.

Using automation software for maximum exposure, you may swap out questions pointing to the same information. Switching up your hashtags increases the likelihood that individuals searching for various subsets of your specialty will see your tweet and click through.

Making presentations from your writing is another option. Numerous visual associations may be made with each item. Create a basic PowerPoint slideshow by considering relevant images to accompany each point in your text. Slideshare should be used to disseminate these PowerPoints. Your slideshows may also be turned into videos with the help of other technologies. You may upload your finished videos to YouTube like any other type of content.

Alternatively, you may transform the points you made in your blog article into visual guides called infographics. Infographics are simplified visual representations of written content like blog posts or news stories. Streamlining your arguments visually draws attention to what's most crucial to the reader. Use Pinterest to spread these infographics.

Finally, you should always choose a captivating header image while publishing content online. A lovely preview will appear when the link is opened on Facebook. It draws attention and motivates individuals to spread its message.

Many different types of content are available for use on Facebook. You may upload and share everything from links to movies, infographics, images, and audio files. After publishing content to your Facebook page, you should distribute the link to that post in groups specifically or broadly interested in your area of expertise.

This is the key to unleashing the potential of recycled materials. Playing the game in this manner necessitates devoting less effort to content creation and more to promotion. Getting your name out there is crucial. Even if your content is excellent, it won't help if no one knows it exists. Ten hours of promotion work should be done for every hour spent on content creation.

This is the proper way to grow your mailing list. Building a solid online identity in this way is essential. Start with impactful content, then make many variations and share them across various social media channels.

CHAPTER 12

Use Automatic Content Sharing

Another incentive to re-purpose your material is highlighted before we move into automated content distribution. Your audience members will likely become disinterested if you repeatedly cover the same ground.

People are hungry for fresh music. They want you to investigate their ancillary requirements. They would rather you refrain from repeating the same ideas repeatedly. That's the type of danger you face if all you do is keep offering folks more of what's already working.

You have discovered the successful content theme. You can see that there is a lot of interest in it. It's no secret that this gets a lot of views. Your need to return to the same topic is understandable. Please don't.

Keep your attention fixed on the most effective means of presenting that idea. Do it only a few times, but put greater emphasis on recycling. In this approach, readers will see that you are discussing topics of interest across several channels. There is a greater possibility that they will listen. The likelihood of their clicking through increases. They're more open to giving things away.

Keep this in mind while you consider other uses. Refrain from assuming that reading Chapter 11 is unnecessary. Not. You want as much of the stuff in your social media feeds to be as popular and engaging as possible.

It would be a tragedy if you figured out what works and stopped caring about anything but the text itself. Unfortunately, there is a limit to what can be accomplished with textual information. This leads me to the topic of automated content sharing. Your hands will be busy if you do this manually since you will be sharing a great deal of stuff; most of it will be from third parties and original and repurposed.

First of all, you have a lot of forms to fill out repeatedly because you will be covering various channels and publishing many different formats on those sites. Even if you have already signed up for these services, the submission process still entails filling out forms. Form completion is required while making a Facebook post.

Assuming you have little material to disseminate, this should be doable. However, you should automate your social media publishing if you want to increase your exposure by posting many times every day.

Unfortunately, it won't help much if you feed data into content publishing systems. The timing of your publication is crucial.

You'd be surprised to learn that most people in your target demographic only log in to their social media accounts (including Facebook, Twitter, Pinterest, and YouTube) during a specific time window every day. You will only reach your core audience if you publish within that window.

It seems promising up to this point. Now, here's the rub: not all audiences are interested simultaneously. But how could you tell? Here is where trying out different things might help.

The first step is to disperse your daily content updates at irregular intervals. Try to spread information at least once an hour. Publish at the top of each hour using content automation technologies. Let things play out for a couple of weeks.

Examine the data once the test time has ended. For instance, Facebook Insights may reveal the peak viewing times for your page's content. With this knowledge in hand, you may adjust the schedule of your automated program to distribute your material during peak hours.

In the beta phase, you could release one piece of content every hour. That's 24 individual bits of material dispersed evenly during 24 hours. You discovered from Facebook Insight that your content is most prevalent between 8 AM and 5 PM. Then, you condense those twenty-four updates into the time frame of eight in the morning to five in the afternoon.

The clustered publication follows these steps. Any intervals of time outside that window can be disregarded. In this approach, you may increase the likelihood that your material will be seen by its intended audience.

Twitter/X-Special Remarks

Repeatedly posting during the best times of day is essential if you use Twitter for publishing. Facebook Insight has previously informed you that people see your posts at certain times. Your Twitter followers probably enjoy the same kind of content on other social networks that you do. Stay within that estimated time.

Here's what happened. The material should be scheduled to be tweeted many times throughout that time range using automated content publishing systems, and various hashtags should be used each time. You may target specific subsets of your specialized market using hashtags that reflect their interests.

Facebook-Specific Remarks

Be bold about re-posting previously published stuff on your Facebook page. Do not publish the same thing more than once. Successful material that has been republished should be sandwiched between pieces of high-quality, selected content.

More eyes will be drawn to your most valuable work in this approach. If they do, you'll have another opportunity to get them to sign up for your mailing list.

Remember that you are giving up traffic in exchange for sharing high-quality material created by others. Although your reputation grows, you cannot attract new email subscribers to your squeeze page. No way is it going to happen. Sharing your unique material increases readers' likelihood of clicking on your recruitment page.

This is why it's crucial to periodically republish your most popular content with other, similarly high-quality pieces of curated content.

CHAPTER 13

Scale Up Your Targeting

Hashtags can be used when posting to social media platforms like Facebook and Twitter. With Instagram, this is undeniably the case. Feel free to experiment with different labels and tags for your material, no matter the medium.

Numerous classifications exist for every specific field. Use them in your experiments. Check the social networking site you're sharing to see which tags generate the most likes or comments.

Of course, you will only discover the ideal hashtags after some time. There's no chance of it occurring. You can only learn this by extensive practice over an extended time frame.

However, a trend should show up in the data from these studies. You'd quickly learn that some hashtags are far more fruitful than others. A lot more people look at them. They are given far more focus. Moreover, they have significantly higher levels of interaction. Don't stray from those.

Try Out Different Methods Of Labelling Influencers In Your Niche

Researching hashtags on Twitter might lead you to influencers who are experts in that particular subject. These folks have an insatiable appetite for posting material on specific topics. Every time they make a post, they always utilize the same handful of hashtags. It appears that is their exclusive preoccupation.

Determine where these individuals are. Read what they have to say. How often are they being retweeted? Is there a lot of interest in what they're offering? Do many people interact with them? Are people reacting on Twitter? You should be able to tell at a glance which accounts have any weight in your field and which do not.

Please avoid getting caught up with the quantity of their fan base. Consider the ratio of their followers to the accounts they follow and the total amount of engagement they receive.

Suppose I discover Mike Smith to be a prominent poster in my niche because he appears to choose from the top ten hashtags for my specialty randomly. In that case, I may investigate the ratio of his followers to the accounts he follows. Mike Smith may be influential if 15,000 people follow him, but only follows one.

I mention this because I need to check how actively people respond to his articles before drawing firm conclusions. Do many people RT his updates? Is there a large amount of feedback? Is the 'love' button getting a lot of use? If his posts have these qualities, they're worth checking out and following.

When posting on Twitter, it is crucial to include notable users. In your article, you use the most effective hashtags you have. This will help them notice you. If you share information comparable to what these individuals like, they will be alerted that you do so.

Don't be shocked if they decide to promote your work to their followers after checking out your job. Talk to them. Get your concerns or ideas over to them. You should interact with them so extensively that they could share your guest articles (if they are bloggers) or talk about your work (if you are active on social media).

When you form a partnership with them, at the absolute least, they join your network of content distributors. Many of these can even land you interviews on popular industry websites.

Refrain from assuming that tagging is the only way to interact with influencers. That's not even the start of it. That's only the beginning of the story. There's so much more they can do to help you. You should constantly interact with them and make conversation.

This in no way necessitates a cheek-to-cheek greeting. It doesn't follow that you must always tell them "Amazing post" or "Great post" in response to their updates. My heart leaps at the thought. No way could work.

Not moving in that direction won't go far enough. It would be best if you gave it some effort. And this might come out as criticism at times. You may come out as unpleasant, but you need to get their attention by doing so. It would be best to convince them that you are an expert in this field and a reputable source of information.

That's how you earn their respect and attention. That's the type of interaction that is sure to make you respected. If you don't stand out, you'll blend in with the rest of the chorus. They need more motivation to include your interview or guest post. For what reason should they? You aren't contributing anything new or offering any perspectives that stand out.

Try Out Some Paid Promotions

Considering buying visitors after you've exhausted all other options, mainly free traffic generation strategies like social media marketing would be best. This may seem excessive, but hear me out.

Initially, you can't predict when your intended readers will see your content. You can only guess at their demographic make-up at first.

How many guys are there in comparison to females in your target demographic? What kinds of articles do men and women like from you? In what age ranges do they fall? When do they come?

I'm hoping you can put this into context. To perform preliminary audience intelligence, you must rely on unpaid traffic. After gaining this knowledge, you may now afford Facebook advertising and those of other platforms.

You will likely waste time and resources if you begin before this stage. Check the numbers first. Observe your audience's behavior closely. Remove any adverts that fit these descriptions.

CHAPTER 14

Sell to Your List Differently

You have successfully converted your social media followers into email subscribers. Feel proud of yourself. You've accomplished something most social media marketers require assistance or don't consider. This is an impressive feat.

It still needs to be simplified to make a mistake even now. Many list members never switch to another list. They consider themselves successful if they can convince enough readers of their blogs to join their mailing lists.

Yes, they are right on some level. You may expect a certain percentage of your list's subscribers to purchase from your affiliate links. Some people on your mailing list will likely purchase your unique works. Others may decide to shop at your virtual wares expo.

The issue, however, is that if you settle with this arrangement, you will be getting pennies on the dollar. In a sense, you are. Do you want to make the most of the time, effort, and resources you put into your business? Why wouldn't you desire the highest possible benefit from your efforts?

You'll need to market your mailing list uniquely to make the most out of your mailing list. There is just no denying it. Any alternative strategy would produce subpar outcomes at best and none at all. Consider these suggestions.

Change up the List of Items You Use

Subscribers may sign up after being inspired by your writing. They are well-versed in the topic at hand. They know what excellent work you produce. They get the points you're trying to make. For this reason, it is illogical for you to include duplicate items on your list.

People aren't stupid, so you may alter the title and rearrange certain things. That won't fool them for a second. They are wise that you give them information they have likely seen previously because of your recycling practices.

Do you believe that this form of training increases self-assurance? Do you think that this approach will result in increased trust being established? Naturally not. You'll need to come up with new material.

Can you describe the required material? First, you don't need us to tell you which posts are the most read on your site. Try these first.

Not in the sense of re-releasing them, though. I mean looking at them critically to identify any discrepancies. Is there anything you still need clarification on? Do the explanations you provided in those viral posts need to be clarified? These ideas should give you a good foundation for the targeted, high-quality material you want to distribute to your subscribers.

Remember that your updates' content is the main draw for your list of subscribers. Your squeeze page's CTA may have been a pricey download, but after your subscribers receive it, they have no reason to continue receiving your emails. Do you get what I'm saying?

Make the reward the revised material you give, and you will be doing yourself a tremendous service. In this way, you may encourage individuals to read your emails and other content regularly. They made your list, so reward them.

Don't let your guard down or allow yourself to get lazy. It's time for you to step into the spotlight. Everything that came before was only practice for this moment. It ends here. This is the point at which everything becomes concrete. And you have to deliver results.

Benefit from Paid Material

Sending out notices to your email list highlighting the material's uniqueness is a sure way to have it go viral. Where do you even begin? Make use of examples from the real world or social proof. These are the words of others who have followed your counsel or had the experiences you describe.

These tales have the power to captivate everybody who reads them. They'll get sucked into the story nonetheless. Your readers will find common ground with the folks giving their tales since they are genuine people. Your mailing list's performance will improve dramatically with such enticing material.

Why? The vast majority of your rivals are only reusing materials. They're taking back their most valuable assets because they know from experience that they work, but they also know that they need to set themselves apart. Taking the easy way out isn't good for their reputation as a company.

It would be best if you decided to alter your approach. This is how you get people to stick with your material over time. Remember that the emails you send out are your material while managing a mailing list.

Try, Try, Try to Make a Sale

The term "upsell" keeps popping into my head. Upselling is essential if you want your mailing list to generate revenue. You don't have to save the day anymore. There's no need to go crazy with this. You needn't put on an air of super-salesmanship.

Most individuals have some idea of how bothersome pushy salespeople can be. In all likelihood, you will resist. You can ignore them and stop receiving them by doing so. I certainly don't blame you. That is the typical reaction of consumers to aggressive salespeople.

What I mean by "upsell" is that you should provide material that draws attention to an issue and suggests a solution. To put it simply, that is upselling. You make individuals aware of the breadth of their problems and the depth of the answers available.

Of course, there are plausible and even better answers to this problem, as there are in most situations. Your mission is to outline conventional solutions that are fine but might be better and to send out email updates that get people interested in finding a solution.

You are directing them toward the optimal answer to their predicament. Use a mailing list for social media advertising. Tell individuals that making picture quotations or video montages out of images is a fantastic answer to their demand for fresh material.

However, an even more ideal approach would be to automate the production of such resources, allowing users to click on photographs and instantly generate a movie. It's a huge time saver, and the finished product would be posted to their social media channels without any more work on their part.

That's the critical difference between adequate solutions and those that stand out better. This is the method of converting leads into subscribers. You are still adding value, answering their questions, and meeting their wants, but you are now presenting them with various alternatives.

They can try to solve the issue independently, as most people would, or they can try something else. When people click on that link to see "something else," that's when you make a sale of an affiliate product, a product of your design, or a service. It's preferable to upsell or upsell regardless of the approach taken.

I wish it were that simple to tell you. This is as easy as outlining several options and emphasizing the best choice. The most significant option, of course, is the one that gives you a cut of the profits from every sale.

It's more complex because there are more moving parts involved. I'll explain why. People join your email list for a variety of reasons. Some visitors are only interested in the freebie but need more initiative to opt out.

You can't seem to shake them. They won't even bother to read your emails. They need more time to read your email messages. You won't see any improvement from them. If there are enough "list squatters" on your email distribution list, your mailing list service will begin charging you extra money each month.

You must employ an open rate filter to remove these people from your list. Again, you'll only be able to reduce its population rather than wipe it out entirely.

Some users on your mailing list may have shown initial enthusiasm but have stopped opening your emails. Even if many people are interested in what you have to say and eagerly await your emails, they can't afford your premium offerings because of the high price tag.

Let me fill you in on a little secret right now. When someone complains that your product or service is "too expensive" or "too unaffordable," they're just trying to tell you that they're not convinced it's worth the cost.

You still have to filter them, though. Either they need more intrinsic motivation to succeed, or you must provide them with sufficient external incentives. Nonetheless, they have yet to make up their minds. Pushing them off the wall is the most incredible option.

In the eyes of a seasoned salesperson, there is no such thing as "unaffordable." There is no difference between selling a $10 product and a $1,000 product if you can talk to someone and convince them that they need to buy your product. You've successfully shifted their perspective from want to need. Therefore, they'll believe that thing.

Individuals put their requirements first. Frequently, their needs are put second to those of others. I hope you get this. I'm assuming you read this. It has nothing to do with the absolute cost of your affiliate product. Instead, you'll need to do some further qualifying or convincing.

This is why more is needed to rely on upselling. The following step, which I will detail below, must be taken.

Apply the Filtering Strategy Based on $1 Lists.

You need to divide your subscriber list into two categories: those who are merely curious and those who will make a purchase. These two communities couldn't be more unlike.

Email opens don't always indicate future purchases. As I noted before, your argument could have been presented better. You may need to provide them with the right qualifications.

To help you appropriately filter your list members, I'll show you a $1 list filtration strategy. Instead of trying to upsell them to more expensive goods (such as those costing $19.95, $34.95, or $349.50), you would set the price of everything on your general list at $1.

What I mean when I say "general list" is the list in which anyone who signs up for your mailing list is included. Your default set of items is here. Please use this broad checklist as a guide. This is the undifferentiated, massive crowd of people considering purchasing your product.

Upselling with $1 incentives allows customers to categorize themselves according to what drives them. Those individuals are enthusiastic enough to spend one dollar. That is to say, they agree with you about the worth of your material and are prepared to back it up monetarily.

Here's what happened. The gap between $1 and paying $100 is not significant. I discovered this the hard way.

When I started doing this, I foolishly assumed that only cheapskates would want to be on my dollar list. They are stingy people. I didn't think they'd go for the big-ticket stuff, at least in my thinking. Oh, how wrong I was!

If a person can mentally overcome the gap between 0 and 1, they can do the same between 1 and 100 with the right amount of exposure and information. This is not a conjecture or hypothesis. This happens right in front of my eyes all the time.

It is up to you to narrow down that long list. When advertising these $1 deals, you challenge potential customers to demonstrate whether or not they are only pretending to be interested. The system is designed to sort itself out. Use it.

People who join your general list likely care about receiving helpful information from you. That's why they exist. However, only a tiny percentage of them would pay for it. This "golden fraction" is what generates profit for you. Your buyer's list is the secret to your financial success.

Once more, a novel approach to list sales is required. This also pertains to your two distinct mailing list categories. Your standard audience receives unique content, including social proof, case studies, and upsell messaging. However, your customer base benefits from higher-value upsells and access to more in-depth content.

Again, if someone is ready to go from zero to one dollar, you can convince them to go from one dollar to one hundred, one thousand dollars, or any other quantity you choose. Keep in mind that the higher the value of the dollar, the lower the conversion rate.

It would be ideal if people separated themselves into groups according to how ready, willing, and eager they were to make a purchase. Since $1 is almost "friction-free," this technique for filtering lists is quite effective.

CHAPTER 15

Reinvest Your Profits the Right Way

You're now making a respectable sum of money monthly from social network traffic thanks to the $1 filtering process. The following action is to establish a company.

You may start thinking of what you're doing now as little more than a pastime. It's a pastime that pays well, but it's still a hobby. That might also be a trap. This can prevent you from reaching the heights of social media traffic success you would otherwise have.

How do you use the knowledge I've given you to build a successful company that will last? It's easy: just put your money back where it belongs.

After you've mastered the system, you may branch out into other areas. Find your market niche with the aid of this education. I have also provided the methods necessary to succeed by leveraging social media visitors. You can afford to dream on a grand scale when you've established a steady income stream from your expertise. Investigating similar niches in addition to your primary focus would be best.

This line of thought is relatively simple. If you've mastered your niche to the point that you're producing passive money every month, you may use your existing method to break into adjacent niches.

That's how you expand your company to new heights. You no longer rely on just one income source; you diversify your earnings from the one method you perfected.

You have mastered the art of social media marketing, from selecting the most relevant hashtags to using effective content presentation and mailing list promotion. Your system incorporates these and many others. It would be a pity to limit the use of that system to a narrow field.

Once you've mastered those, you can branch out into similar subjects. The most effective list marketers use many lists. It's one of several they run. And it means six- or even seven-figure salaries every year. Your success is inevitable if theirs is.

Spend more money on targeted clicks once you've determined what's practical.

Once you've figured out what kind of content marketing plan performs best on Facebook, you may invest in qualified leads. How? Use Facebook's "look-alike" feature to reach new individuals who share your audience's interests. This is the reason why Facebook rocks. This is also the cause of their legal troubles.

The moment you go onto Facebook, whether you want to believe it or accept it, it spies on you. It takes into account your preferences and comments, as well as those of your friends, to make educated guesses about your future actions and tastes. As such, it builds a profile of your interests based on the content you've indicated you enjoy.

Using Facebook's look-similar audience technology, you may identify new potential followers who share the same interests as your present followers but have yet to visit your page. Wow, that's some impressive gadgetry. Use this to your advantage. You may advertise in front of people more likely to be interested in your brand.

Increase Your Spending on Unique Material

Creating unique material is an option worth considering. You may take your business to the next level if it is already profitable by providing additional value to the people who follow your brand across various social media platforms and on your blog or website by creating unique content.

This means you can start banging out articles later. You can get somebody good at writing to do it for you. Thanks to worldwide outsourcing, websites like ozki.org can provide high-quality, unique content without breaking the bank. Superior content that keeps readers interested should stay within your bottom line.

Spend money on regularly updated content. This piece of advice naturally follows from the last one I made. If you want to spend more money on original material, you will also spend more on expanded content updates. More of what you create will be uniquely yours.

You can only do one with the other. Whatever the case, you must improve your content update frequency to provide more value.

In the early stages of implementing this framework, you will likely be interested in affiliate sales if you follow the instructions in this tutorial. You enroll in an affiliate program and then promote your affiliate link in regular email newsletters. You'll earn a commission when someone follows the link and purchases an item. Easy to understand and follow.

If you're serious about financial independence, you should abandon affiliate marketing. You do. You'll need to market your wares instead. The main reason you should do this is for control purposes. When reselling the work of others, you are at their squeeze pages, landing pages, and, ultimately, the product's mercy.

Okay, but what if their stuff stinks? What if their landing page only converts a small percentage of visitors? That's a bad break for you. That's what it comes down to. You should put your money into your creative works if you value financial independence.

You can always rely on outsourcing, which is excellent news. Professional content producers like ozki.org and others may assist you in creating unique, high-quality content for pennies on the dollar.

Create and Market Your Video Membership Courses to Sell

The primary issue with online goods sales is that you only make a sale once. The transaction is finalized when a customer selects the "buy" button, completes payment, and receives the download link. They have the item already. They are free to take, use, or discard it as they see fit.

However, this was a one-time deal. Getting regular monthly payments from kind individuals would be fantastic, wouldn't it? Wouldn't it be amazing if you had a steady stream of money coming in? And that's precisely what you get when you start charging for your online video courses.

If you run a gardening blog, you could create a video-based course in which you instruct others on how to grow a garden. A certain amount is automatically deducted from each member's PayPal or credit card every month. Nothing at all is required of you. And it keeps happening every month until they finally give up and cancel.

Intriguing, right? The videos only require one shoot, yet they continue to bring in cash month after month. That's cool. Income that doesn't need active effort is termed passive income.

The best part is that you are open to more than just video. It might be for any club or organization. You may provide them with access to images. You could grant them access to a set of files or some software.

They are paying for the privilege of downloading the content repeatedly each month. That's a crucial part. The end aim must be a steady stream of money. How to get the most out of your efforts. The less effort you put in, the more money the system rewards you.

This is not something you will be able to master immediately. It also only occurs slowly. Please put your time and effort into the preceding stages initially.

Conclusion

Many people need help with social media marketing. You'll be in trouble if you allow the urban legends around it. This lesson reveals a tried-and-true strategy for converting your online following into actual, tangible dollars.

I'm not saying it's simple, but it is possible to follow these instructions. Do what it says, try different things, and zero down on what works.

The goal is to adapt this knowledge to your situation to develop specific, doable strategies for generating genuine passive income. It would be best to continue once you've mastered the current level.

Now that you have access to all the resources you need remember that it won't do you any good to keep this knowledge to yourself. No way, no how, never, ever. They need action on your part. A sense of urgency is necessary to turn this information into action. The longer you think about it, the less likely your financial situation will improve.

Set a deadline for yourself. Set a precise date to get started. Begin at once as that time arrives. You don't have to save the world or smash a grand slam on your first try. Even a baby step in the right direction is better than none.

Why? Even the smallest of victories is cause for celebration. It would be best if you persisted in this. You need to proceed methodically. Nothing about your current mood or which side of the bed you woke up on is relevant. The most important thing is that you stay the course.

The key to success is dedication and single-mindedness. I hope and pray that you achieve enormous success. The training you just saw was beneficial.

www.ingramcontent.com/pod-product-compliance
Lightning Source LLC
LaVergne TN
LVHW100326210926
848480LV00003B/1277
9798349534669